How to Ask for a Raise

RUSS HOVENDICK

Faithful Life Publishers & Printers
North Fort Myers, FL 33903

FaithfulLifePublishers.com

Copyright © 2012 Russ Hovendick

ISBN: 978-1-937129-40-8

Directional Motivation, LLC.
5421 W 41st #202
Sioux Falls, SD 57106

(605) 362-8176 ext 101
russ@directionmotivation.com

Published and printed by:
Faithful Life Publishers & Printers
3335 Galaxy Way
North Fort Myers, FL   33903

888.720.0950

www.FaithfulLifePublishers.com
info@FLPublishers.com

Printed in the United States of America.

18 17 16 15 14 13 12   1 2 3 4 5

TABLE OF CONTENTS

ACKNOWLEDGMENTS

I've been thinking about this book for many years. My sincere thanks to Millie Lapidario for helping me convert my thoughts to paper. Your encouragement and insight were invaluable through the process. Thank you to Robin Ludwikowski for sharing her keen insights from the Fortune 500 Human Resource perspective. This allowed me to balance the book with differing viewpoints from the employer and employee. Also, a special thank you to my son, Darin, for his patience, wisdom, and positive reinforcement through the writing process.

INTRODUCTION

Are you racking your brains out, trying to boost your income? Are you looking for a magic formula or secret negotiating tactic? I'll tell you now: There is none. The key is transforming your perspective and attitude. This book is unique in that it will challenge you to push yourself professionally and understand how your employer views the topic of salary.

As a recruiter for two decades, I hear stories about employees asking for raises all the time. My job puts me in the unique position to hear the behind-the-scenes drama from both sides. On one hand, I'll listen to a boss explain everything the employee did wrong. And on the other hand, I'll listen to a nervous, frustrated worker wondering how his request for a salary bump could have possibly been rejected.

After 20 years of hearing about employees making the same mistakes time after time when asking for a raise, I'm just itching to tell you what I know! Let me help. Listening to these stories is like watching the same predictable horror flick where the person being chased by the knife-yielding maniac runs *inside* the house. If you've ever yelled at that character from your sofa, you know how I feel.

Let me explain: I want everyone who truly deserves a raise to get one. I've been there before, sitting in my boss's office, sweating bullets and saying all the wrong things out of nervousness. (A conversation about salary is the worst time to suffer from diarrhea of the mouth.) But I've grown in my career and come to a point where workers ask me for raises. I'm also privy to stories from hundreds of clients through the years, and I've learned that asking for a raise is not as difficult as it seems.

Your inner skeptic might say, *Oh Russ, but you haven't met my boss. He's an irrational, mean-spirited, bullheaded dictator. He does not respond to reason!* Granted, bosses come in all personality types and depending on your boss's temperament, the mere thought of approaching that topic could make you nauseous.

Before we go any further, you must understand and accept the three major principles of this book:

1) Getting a raise is less about your boss and work environment than it is about you. Ultimately, it is your employer's decision whether or not you get that salary increase. However, you determine your worth. You control the value you hold in the company.

2) Proving your value comes before asking for a raise.

3) Asking for a raise is a process—not a one-time event.

Take a moment to reflect on these three ideas.

But Russ, my boss sets the pay, not me! How can you say it's more about me than my boss?

But Russ, my work speaks for itself. Why do I have to prove anything?

But Russ, if asking for a raise is a "process," then how long will it be before I get the raise I deserve?

For now, let's let your inner skeptic take a break. All that nay-saying can get tiresome, right? Just be open to accepting these principles and as you read my step-by-step instructions, these principles will make perfect sense.

You also need to get over some preconceived notions about asking to earn higher wages. Why cloud your head with unsubstantiated judgments? Don't give fodder to the voice inside that prevents you from getting ahead.

The Three Myths of Pursuing a Raise

Myth No. 1: Employers hate giving raises.
Truth: Employers usually tell me exactly the opposite. I've witnessed workers manage to get raises from companies that were either struggling financially or had policies limiting raises to once a year. I've also seen individuals score salary increases that exceeded pay grades. Most employers are willing to reward top performers who add value to the company. When bosses recognize that value, they want to keep you motivated and part of the team.

Myth No. 2: Only brownnosers and suck-ups get raises.
Truth: Although it happens, the truth is that employers pay for performance. The volume and quality of your work directly translates

into the company's bottom line. It always helps to cultivate a cordial relationship with your boss, but if the only thing you can do well is kiss butt, you're probably not going to get a raise.

Myth No. 3: Asking for a raise will get you fired.
Truth: If you go into a salary discussion with a respectful and professional manner, there is no way your boss will want to fire you. I promise! The tools in this book will guide you on the proper method to approach the topic. The worst that can happen is you don't get your raise this time. But it may lead to a promotion and salary increase in the near future if you follow the steps in this book.

There is no fool-proof, 100% satisfaction guaranteed method of getting a raise. If I told you this book would undoubtedly boost your income, I would be a liar. The process I detail in this book is the best way to maximize your chances of increasing your salary.

I strongly recommend reading it with a pen and notebook handy, so you can take notes and journal your ideas and plans. I also suggest that you read the entire book before approaching your boss to discuss your salary. You can also go to our website www.directionalmotivation.com and download complimentary worksheets tailored for this book.

Whether you're at your first job still struggling with how to talk to your boss at all or whether you're an experienced professional with no qualms about talking to your boss, this book offers golden advice.

So while I cannot promise you will get a raise after following my advice, I can guarantee you this:
- You'll have a new perspective on your role in the company.

- You'll have new tools you can use in other negotiations.

- You'll communicate more effectively with your boss.

- Your boss will respect your approach.

Is the inner skeptic fast asleep now? Have you deleted these three myths from the hard drive of your brain? Excellent. Now it's time to focus.

CHAPTER 1
Don't Let This Happen to You

Let me start by telling you a story about an employee named Jessica Hightstown. She was fresh out of college and concluded that she deserved a raise. This is what happened:

Jessica had spent eight days agonizing over how to approach her boss. Shirley Jackson, an intimidating figure, was the head of marketing and the epitome of the savvy, overachieving businesswoman. She walked briskly with perfect posture and typically had three or four people chasing after her with questions, updates or documents to sign.

On this Tuesday morning, Jessica spent her morning commute rehearsing her case for a raise. When Jessica arrived at the office, she plopped herself outside Shirley's office. *I don't want to bother her, so I'll just wait,* Jessica thought. *But it will happen as soon as that door opens. Be brave! Shirley's usually pretty nice.*

Five long minutes later, the door remained shut. Coworkers walked by and Jessica smiled politely. Shirley's office abutted the cubicle area and was only several feet from the water cooler. The normal buzz of phones ringing, faxes arriving and office chatter filled the air. Jessica thought, *Since I'm waiting, I might as well check my Facebook page.*

Thirty-two minutes later, Jessica saw the knob start to turn. *It's now or never. It's taken me this long, so there's no going back. Do it! Do it!*

The door opened and Shirley was in mid-step, arms wrapped around a three-inch thick pile of papers. She had been deeply immersed in whatever she was reading. Her eyeglasses perched at the edge of her nose.

"Shirley, can we talk?" Jessica called out. *Can't let her get away! I've got to catch her now or else she'll be stuck in meetings all day.*

"Oh, good morning, Jessica," Shirley said. She had always been gracious and accommodating, but at this moment, her eyebrows were furrowed more than usual. Shirley kept her head down and moved only her eyes in Jessica's direction. She remained standing outside her office door. "Is everything alright?"

"Well, ah yes . . . and no, I guess," Jessica said. She then waited for Shirley to say something, but a few seconds of awkward silence had already set in. *Quick, say something!* "I mean, well, . . . ugh . . . I need a raise."

Several heads popped up above the cubicle walls. The cubicle workers heard loud and clear and exchanged glances.

"Well, Jessica, this isn't a good time," replied Shirley, noticeably surprised. *Why now?* Shirley thought. *I just got out of an hour-long conference call and need to cram before the big presentation this afternoon! And why here? We're practically in the lobby.* "I'm not in a position to discuss this."

"Yes, I understand. Let's go to your office. It will only take a minute," Jessica said. *Stay firm,* Jessica told herself.

But Shirley didn't budge. She stood in the same spot outside her office, waiting for Jessica to move out of the way.

"You see, I was thinking on the drive over this morning that I have already been here for two months, only late a couple of times, and do just as much work as everyone else here."

Two months? She hasn't even completed her 90-day probation period, Shirley thought.

"Besides, I am only making $1,700 a month. I'm sure others make more."

Shirley remained silent. Her head tilted down toward her papers while her eyes studied Jessica. *This girl is embarrassing herself. She needs to stop talking right now.*

"I just bought a car," Jessica said. "So I need $200 more per month just to cover my payments."

And how is this relevant? Shirley thought. She remained silent.

Just then, Bill Meyers, Vice President of Operations came around the corner. He told Shirley he needed to quickly brief her on an account change. The client was waiting for her in the main lobby.

"I'll be right there, Bill," Shirley said, motioning for him to walk ahead. Before leaving, she glared quickly at Jessica and said, "You're right. We need to talk. Please be in my office at 11 a.m. sharp." Shirley sped away, leaving Jessica standing alone with a sudden headache. Her knees felt weak. Several feet away, chuckles erupted from behind the cubicles.

What just happened? Or worse, what is going to happen? Jessica returned to her desk, avoiding eye contact with her colleagues. She could not concentrate on the pile of documents waiting to be processed.

All she could do was watch the clock and replay what felt like the longest conversation she'd had with Shirley. She envisioned Shirley's stern glare. *What have I done?* She could no longer subdue her panic. She burst into tears and sank her head face down on her desk.

Poor Jessica had no clue. She later found out that she had violated company policy by discussing her salary in front of others. Jessica could have easily been fired for her reckless approach.[1]

Did Jessica's last name, Hightstown, ring a bell? I named her after the Hightstown rail accident in 1833 because her story is a train wreck. Her approach went from bad to worse. It may sound like a fictional story created to highlight her many jaw-dropping missteps. But you'd be surprised at how common her story is.

We—including yours truly—have all made foolish mistakes in our careers. You can start out with the best intentions such as "I want to take control of my career." But the more you try to reach that goal, you hype it up and the plan goes haywire. Don't let this happen to you.

---

1 At this early stage, I issue a word of caution: Do not tell any coworkers that you are planning to ask for a raise. This rule is non-negotiable and I will explain more on this in Chapter 3.

CHAPTER 2
Your Employer: The Consumer

Let's continue imagining Shirley, the quintessential boss. She analyzes and stores information in her head like a bottomless pit. When shopping for electronics, her ritual is even more precise. It starts with reading expert ratings, then consumer ratings, and lastly, price comparisons among multiple retailers.

On Shirley's latest search for a PC laptop, she compares models and brands methodically. Brand A's $1,500 model has the same basic features as her old laptop she bought a couple of years ago for $700: 4GB of memory and a 320GB hard drive.

On the other hand, Brand B's $1,500 model has 8GB of memory, a 500GB hard drive and a faster processor. Is there even a slight possibility that Shirley would pick Brand A?

The answer is clear because we are all consumers. We are all looking to get the most bang for our buck. If Shirley paid $1,500 for a laptop with no more than the same features she already had, she'd be a sorry fool. She knew the value of the Brand A laptop was much lower than its sticker price.

All employers are consumers. You are the merchandise. You create your value.

Russ, how dare you call me "merchandise." I'm a unique individual.

I know my statement can sound disconcerting to some, but the sooner you understand your employer's point of view, the easier it will be for you to get into the right mindset to get that raise!

Your boss is a consumer. Repeat after me: My boss is a consumer.

That doesn't mean she is a cold-hearted, money hungry, swindler. It means that setting an employee's salary is the equivalent of purchasing an item. Your boss asks the same questions you ask when shopping:

- What am I getting for my money?

- Is it worth it?

- If I buy this item, what will it do for me?

When you've discovered that the price of an item you buy regularly has gone up, what do you do? You ask what has changed about the product. You ask what additional benefits come with the higher price tag. If there are no additional benefits, you'd likely search in another store. After all, if the product is still the same old product, what is the rationale in paying a higher price?

This is exactly what your employer is considering when you ask for a raise. She may not ask explicitly, but it is your responsibility to clearly demonstrate your value. In the story in Chapter 1, Jessica made grave mistakes from beginning to end. Her fundamental flaw, however, was that she never demonstrated her value.

CHAPTER 3
Assess Yourself

Most of the time, employees think the hard part is meeting with the boss. But the real work begins at taking a thorough, accurate personal assessment. This is where you take a step back and analyze your job performance objectively and truthfully. The assessment answers the question "Do I deserve a raise?"

Of course I deserve a raise. That's why I bought this book!

Yes, I understand that. But I still cannot stress enough the importance of this first step. Sigmund Freud once said, "Being entirely honest with oneself is a good exercise." In this case, the self-assessment not only helps you examine your strengths and weaknesses at work. It also helps you prepare the case you will present to your boss.

Keep in mind that nobody is looking over your shoulder. This is not the time to boost your ego, impress anyone, or rationalize your weaknesses. You must be totally, unabashedly honest with yourself. Think of this activity as an internal fact-finding mission.

Remember this: You're in a good position. You're employed. You're doing this out of your free will. You're assessing yourself with the intent of coming out the other end a brighter, more motivated, and focused professional.

Personal Assessment Part I

Let's warm up with a few general questions. Using the worksheet below, rate yourself on a scale of 1 to 5. Check off your scores to each question. The following assessments can also be downloaded and printed from our website, www.directionalmotivation.com.

Attitude
Rate your desire to please your boss.

	1.	What for? He/She is a jerk!
	2.	I do my job. He should be pleased with that.
	3.	I do what I can to help my boss. I don't know if I'm pleasing my boss.
	4.	I do my best to help my boss. I hope he is pleased.
	5.	I enjoy doing the legwork for my boss. I learn a lot.

Rate your willingness to help your colleagues.

	1.	Why should I help anyone? No one helps me!
	2.	If the boss is watching, then sure, I'm willing to help.
	3.	I assist my colleagues if I am able to do so and if I have time.
	4.	I enjoy helping my colleagues.
	5.	I take pride in doing extra work to make everybody else's jobs easier.

Teamwork

What is your perspective on working with others?

	1.	My teammates are a big hassle. I refuse to work with them.
	2.	If it means less work for each person, then it makes sense to work together.
	3.	I prefer to work alone, but if I have to, I will force myself to work with them.
	4.	It works out if everyone does one's assigned tasks.
	5.	The best part of belonging to a team is that each person contributes one's greatest strengths.

How do you contribute to your team?

	1.	I am cautious of other people taking credit for my work, so I avoid contributing. But if I have a juicy story about a colleague from another department, I will contribute that for entertainment purposes.
	2.	I wait until others offer their help before I start offering my help.
	3.	I share my knowledge with the team.
	4.	I spend extra time researching information for the team.
	5.	I inspire the people around me to do better.

Work Volume & Quality

Describe how you handle the workload and deadlines.

	1.	My boss puts too much work on me. I need a break right now.
	2.	My deadlines are too tight. I just finish when I finish.
	3.	I meet deadlines, but sometimes sacrifice quality. Or I sacrifice deadlines for quality.

	4.	I sometimes struggle with both the demands of the job, but I give each project my all.
	5.	I developed a system that keeps me on top of my work, and I communicate with my manager regularly.

What is the first thing you do when customers or clients go to your workstation?

	1.	I pretend I'm on the phone, so they take a hint and don't bother me.
	2.	I try to find another colleague who can help them.
	3.	I take down their requests and hope it gets done.
	4.	I take down their requests and put it on my to-do list.
	5.	I smile and ask what I can do to help them with a genuine intention of doing so. I also confirm that I understand them correctly and prioritize when to execute the task.

Knowledge & Skills

To what extent are you expanding your knowledge and skills?

	1.	If my boss wanted me to learn more, why didn't she tell me?
	2.	I don't have time to go through any more training.
	3.	I am open to exploring more about my industry.
	4.	I read industry publications and blogs once in a while to keep me updated.
	5.	I constantly seek more information through classes, workshops, webinars and more. There is always more to learn.

Attendance & Punctuality

Tell me about how often you're absent or tardy.

	1.	I don't keep track. No one notices whether or not I'm there anyway.
	2.	I come in 15 minutes late a few times a week. It's not my fault. I live the farthest away from the office.
	3.	I come in 15 minutes early, clock in, then mosey on down to the coffeemaker and chat for a while with my colleagues about the weather.
	4.	I come in on time most of the time.
	5.	I appreciate that my boss allows me to come in early. It gives me extra quiet time in the morning to get more done.

Now answer the questions again except this time, rate the top performer in your department. By "top performer," I don't mean the kiss butt. I mean the standout guy, the "it" girl, the one whose name makes the top of every list you wish you could make. This is the person people flock to because of the energy that surrounds him or her. Where flies might surround the company's dead weight, butterflies and harp music surround the top performer. You'll typically hear this person's name around the office in the following sentences: *He did it again!* or *What is her secret?* The top performer consistently works hard and can turn garbage to gold.

Attitude

Rate his/her desire to please the boss.

1   2   3   4   5

Rate his/her willingness to help his/her colleagues.

1   2   3   4   5

Teamwork

Rate how well he/she works with others.

1   2   3   4   5

Rate how much he/she contributes to the team.

1   2   3   4   5

Work Volume & Quality

Rate how he/she handles the workload and deadlines.

1   2   3   4   5

What is the first thing he/she does when customers or clients go to his/her workstation?

_____

_____

_____

_____

_____

_____

_____

Knowledge & Skills

To what extent is he/she expanding his/her knowledge and skills?

1   2   3   4   5

Attendance & Punctuality

1   2   3   4   5

Personal Assessment Part II

Are you starting to see how it all comes back to attitude? Your attitude is the No. 1 factor influencing your job performance, which translates into your ability to boost your income. I promise I'm not saying this in the same way my seventh grade teacher used to scold me for having an "attitude problem." I'm merely trying to show you that you have the power to change your situation by starting with your attitude.

We are creatures of habit. If the habits we form are based on a poor attitude, all future performance will be based on this.

Look at the typical cycle I see everywhere.

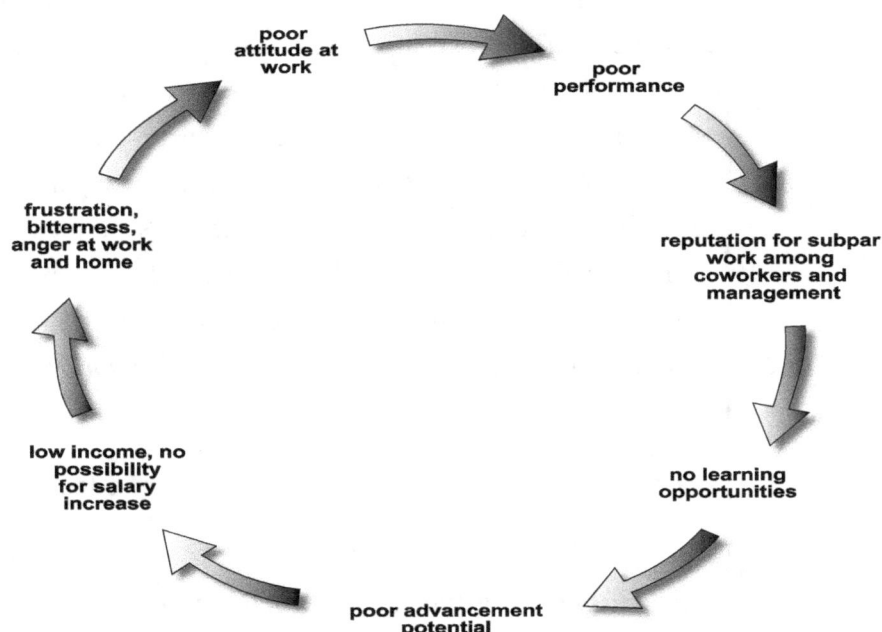

Wow, attitude has that big of an effect on my income and life overall? You bet it does. But don't take my word for it. Meet my cast of characters below and see how their attitudes work for them.

Bitter Brian constantly broods over getting paid less than his colleague Randy. In Brian's opinion, Randy is a preppy brownnoser. When the boss asks for volunteers to manage a new project that would require an extra several hours of work per week for the next month, Brian looks down to the ground, thinking to himself, *Let Randy do it. He gets paid more than me.*

Randy takes the project, works longer hours for the next month and develops new marketing skills he can add to his resume and clips for his portfolio. Meanwhile, Brian continues to leave the office at 5 p.m. sharp, as always.

Above-it-all Abby is a bright and experienced paralegal. In her previous job, she held a senior paralegal position and was assigned to prepare reports involving some juicy court cases. As luck would have it, Abby was laid off and found another paralegal job. At her new firm, she happily takes on research-related duties, but when her supervisor asks her to collect signatures for contracts or pick up coffee, Abby manages to duck those requests. While she's smiling and making up excuses, she's thinking, *I'm too smart for this crap! I deserve a promotion and a raise!*

Her supervisor starts to notice the pattern and feels she cannot rely on Abby.

Rigid Rachel, a purchasing manager for 20 years, memorizes every word of her job description. At least that's what her coworkers think because of her common response.

"Rachel, there is a conference this weekend and I'd like you to attend."

"It's not in my job description."

"Rachel, we need to develop a training course for the new inventory clerks."

"It's not in my job description."

"Rachel, we need start looking into new purchasing software."

"It's not in my job description."

Everybody eventually learns not to approach Rachel with new ideas.

Chairwarmer Charlie is an accounting clerk. He works hard on Mondays because that's a heavy invoice day. But he works even harder at memorizing his supervisor's schedule. When she's out, Charlie passes the time playing Tetris or Bejeweled on his computer. He reserves Solitaire for the last 20 minutes of the day. On Fridays, he removes pennies from his jar of paperclips. If time permits, he may even separate the jumbo paper clips from the mini paper clips.

The one thought that occupies his mind at the office: *I'm bored. Is it time to go home yet?*

Do you see yourself in any of these characters? I admit it: I've been one of these characters at some point in my career. If you were supervising Charlie, Rachel, Abby or Brian, would you feel inclined to give any of them a raise?

Personal Assessment Part III

Gather some reference materials to help you put what you have discovered so far into perspective. Anything that describes your responsibilities and highlights your role in the company will be helpful:

- job description
- company organizational chart
- your past performance evaluations (If you have none so far, obtain the performance evaluation template from your employer.)
- work log if you keep one

If you don't already have these materials, ask your manager, supervisor, department head or someone from human resources. If they ask why you need it, just tell the truth: You are evaluating your job performance. There is no need to tell anyone that you're planning to ask for a raise at this point.

Read these materials and see if they give you more clarity. Go through each responsibility and duty from your job description. Write down what you've done right and what you need to improve on.

Make sure to write down or type your answers.

You're not getting *the* most out of this exercise if you're simply answering them internally. We tend to have a photographic memory. By physically getting the words onto a page, you're ingraining the images of those words into your memory.

You'll be happy you did this when you're sitting in your boss's office about to shed some light on your pay situation. Instead of letting your nerves take over, you'll eloquently explain your assessment to the boss.

Know your employer's priorities.

Do your accomplishments reflect the company's priorities? Allow me to tell a quick story about Susie, a bank teller. She is incredibly proud that after working there for many years, her cash balances have stayed at a whopping high accuracy rate of 99%. In other words, she almost never makes mistakes when accepting or distributing cash. She takes great pride in her excellent rate of accuracy.

However, her bank places a higher priority in sales. Recent policy changes dictate that tellers must sell and cross-sell the bank's products. Susie disagrees with the policy because she sees her function more as customer service rather than sales.

If she were to ask for a raise based on the fact that her accuracy rate is high—while her sales numbers are low—she'd be making a big mistake. The value Susie sees in her accuracy rate is actually quite small compared to the company's value placed on sales. Susie has not evolved to the changing job requirements. Worse yet, she has no intention to do so. By ignoring her employer's priorities, Susie is putting her future with the bank at jeopardy. Are you making the adjustments required for your position?

Answer the questions below. Think about each question deeply and keep writing until you've exhausted the question. Don't concern yourself with grammar or spelling. Simply write. Consider these answers as private as a diary.

1) What do you consider a successful workday? How closely does this resemble what your boss would say for your position?

2) What do you consider a successful workweek? How closely does this resemble what your boss would say for your position?

3) How well do you balance quantity and quality of work?

4) Are you proud of your work? Why or why not?

5) Do you inspire your team members? How so? If not, how do you influence your team?

6) If I asked your coworkers to describe your reputation, what do you think they would say? What words would they use to describe you as a fellow colleague?

7) How well do you communicate with your clients, coworkers and superiors? Do you seek clarification?

8) In what situations have you gone above and beyond the expectations of the position?

9) How often do you offer to help without being instructed to do so?

10) How easily do you adapt to changing situations?

11) Think about your decision-making process at work. How well do you make decisions?

12) Where do you excel?

13) What are your weak points?

14) Now go over your answers to No. 13 and consider the following:

- Is being deficient in these areas normal at this stage of your career?

- Have you had the proper training to address those weak points? If not, you should remember to ask for training during your upcoming conversation with the boss.

By now, you should have a more holistic view of your work performance, work ethic, and role in the company. Review your answers as if you were the boss. If these were your employee's answers, would you agree this person deserves a raise?

If yes, you're ready to move on to the next step. If not, you can still move on to the next steps. However, instead of asking for a raise, you will ask for a plan to help you increase your salary in the future.

CHAPTER 4
Do Your Research

The fact-finding mission continues. You have already demonstrated your bravery in the previous chapter by writing down your successes and failures. By now, you've developed a more intimate understanding of yourself as an employee and perhaps a more realistic view of how others might view you.

You know you deserve a raise, but for how much? How do you determine that amount? What evidence do you present to the boss to support that?

Remember Jessica from Chapter 1? All she knew was that she needed enough money to pay for her new car. And she had an inkling that her coworkers earned more than she did.

You are exponentially more intelligent than Jessica. You determine the amount—and will justify it—through research. Find the salary range for someone with your job title in your local area. Explore your company's financial condition. Find your company's policies on salary raises and whether it has plans for growth or layoffs. Any information that will support your case for a raise will help you.

Do you feel swamped with all the extra work ahead? Don't fret! The Internet makes this type of research much easier than it was for previous generations. The public—that means you—has the power to be totally informed. Take advantage of that. If you are genuinely interested in finding the information, you will have the energy to dig for it. Curiosity will charge your battery. And why wouldn't you be curious about your own industry?

Imagine yourself as a journalist, a private investigator or a covert CIA agent. Digging up information can be grueling or fun. You might as well pick the latter.

WARNING: Do not discuss this with your coworkers.

I understand the urge to share your plans with a coworker. You might know a coworker everyone considers a walking encyclopedia for much of the needed information. Also, seeking comfort in camaraderie is perfectly natural. After all, who knows your work troubles better than your cubicle buddy, right?

Resist all temptation to tell a coworker. Once that information leaves your mouth, you have no control over where it travels and how it's delivered throughout the office. You risk gaining the reputation of "the disgruntled employee" among your peers, which could ruin your credibility and keep others away. You might end up pitting people against each other by carelessly throwing around salary figures. In most corporate cultures, discussing compensation with an associate is grounds for termination.

But what if I make my friend pinky swear not to tell a living soul?

Really? The possibility of losing your job isn't enough to convince you to keep quiet? Consider this hypothetical situation:

You're a mile deep in work and you're at your desk feeling overwhelmed. When you go home tonight, you'll have to spend a few hours digging up the information detailed in this chapter. Your cubicle buddy Marge senses you are tense and invites you to happy hour at the bar across the street.

"No, I really shouldn't," you say. "I have too much to do."

"But your shift ends in 10 minutes! What more is there to do?"

You smile politely, trying to avoid eye contact.

"Come on, honey, loosen up! You need a break. Just one drink. My treat."

"Thank you. I just can't though."

"What's wrong? Are you okay?"

"I'm fine, really."

"Something's up. I can tell."

You look Marge in the eye and she is smiling, patiently waiting for you to unburden whatever is troubling you. She's such a great friend. You've known her for five years and have lunch together almost every day. You hesitate for a moment, feeling guilty because Marge tells you everything, including her money woes.

"You promise not to tell anybody?" you succumb to your inclination.

"Of course."

In a hushed voice, you tell her everything. She praises you and even advises you on where to look for information. You instantly feel uplifted.

Three days later, you haven't finished researching and your boss calls you into his office.

"Word around here has it that you are not happy," he says. "I think we need to talk."

A number of things could have happened. Someone might have overheard the conversation. Or Marge might have accidentally let it slip to another coworker, Brandon, and although she swore him to secrecy, Brandon spilled the secret to Rudy. And on and on, the secret spread like wildfire.

Don't let this happen to you.

How much are you worth?

Your market value

On our website directionalmotivation.com we have a salary calculator that allows you to run a free report showing the typical salary range for positions equal or similar to yours in your area. Salary.com and Payscale.com both have paid options to generate more detailed reports. For example, when you pay for a report, you can submit information on years of experience, skills, level of education, and job responsibilities in order to find the salary range of people similar to you.

A free and useful resource is the Occupational Outlook Handbook, available online from the U.S. Department of Labor Bureau of Labor Statistics. The comprehensive report, revised every two years, lists hundreds of positions and provides details such as education and training, job outlook and median annual wages. Keep in mind that wages vary greatly among regions.

Competency level and qualifications of others in your position

Be creative with this one. You might be able to get information from a local recruiter. Look through job listings for positions similar to yours. Find what qualifications, level of education, and general professional background are most sought after for these positions. If those positions pay more than your current salary and you meet or exceed those qualifications, congratulations, you've found one major piece of supporting evidence.

Your company's salary policies

Dig through your employee handbook and any other company documents that contain information on salaries. Recall conversations you might have had with your boss or human resources representative when you first took the position. Did you keep any notes?

Check whether there are company policies on the following:

1) Minimum length of employment before getting a raise, such as the probation period. Probation periods are typically 90 days. Don't ask for a raise within your probation period. Your employer is still learning about you.

2) Pay grades within each department. Government jobs are the most transparent about pay grades.

3) Specified achievements required before salary increases such as sales figures, test scores, licensing requirements, etc.

Financial health of your company

This can be a little tricky depending on the company's openness on this topic and the availability of public records on your employer. Financial records for government agencies and large corporations are easier to find than those for small private companies. It's easy to get bogged down digging up this information, so I offer a few methods:

1) Listen, listen and observe. When your senses are heightened, you'd be surprised at how much useful information is floating around in the office. You know that buzz you try to tune out when you're concentrating? Allow yourself to absorb it. Imagine you are a sponge. Let's say you hear the lab technicians talking about the company's recent $50,000 purchase for a special microscope. Let's say you overhear an administrative assistant grumbling about the rush to print 15 new hire packets and employee handbooks. New hires and high-priced equipment purchases mean the company can afford them. Of course, use common sense here and be cautious of gaining a reputation as an eavesdropper.

2) Strike up a conversation here and there. Do you know anyone in the sales or finance departments? Ask them how they're doing. Nudge the conversation into how the company is doing financially. What do they see as the company's biggest challenges? Is the company facing some steep competition? How do we compare to the competitors? How well is the company doing in the marketplace?

These prodding conversations don't have to be limited to sales or finance. Other staffers in operations, for example, might have some insights into whether they've heard of upcoming layoffs or new building expansions.

Everyone in the office can potentially be a valuable source of information. Don't be shy. People generally like to be asked for their opinions. When you ask open-ended questions, you allow the other person to expound. Just remember to act naturally and be polite. More importantly, don't allow this to distract you from work. You will still have to prove why you deserve the raise.

Use financial information services online. Bloomberg News provides comprehensive financial snapshots for businesses worldwide, including the latest news stories, stock prices and income statements from the previous quarter. Google Finance and Yahoo! Finance also provide stock information and the latest news stories. However, information on small companies that are not publicly traded is typically not available on these sites.

Go to the U.S. Securities and Exchange Commission website. The SEC has a search engine called the Next-Generation EDGAR System that allows you to search a company's corporate reports simply by typing in the company name. The website also includes helpful beginner guides on financial statements and corporate reports.

3) If your employer is a government agency, go to its website. You should find a listing of salary ranges and the annual budget. Most local government agencies have a public information officer to assist you in finding this information.

Beware of the dark hole you may fall into if you overdo the research. Do not waste time and lose momentum. Periodically ask yourself whether you have enough information to support your case for a raise. If you were the boss, would this information be enough to convince you to give your employee a raise? If not, what else would you need to know?

CHAPTER 5
Prepare for the Meeting

If you've completed the first two steps thoroughly, consider yourself an expert on the following topics: you as an employee, your value in the company, your financial worth in the marketplace, your company's pay policies and your company's financial status. You're significantly more knowledgeable about these topics than you were when you first started. Now you must prepare how you will deliver your message and convince your boss that you deserve a raise.

You're entering the critical stages of the process. How do you feel? Like a soldier going into battle? A fighter walking into the ring? I hope not! I want you to be confident, but above all, know that it comes down to the three P's: Preparation, Presentation and above all, Professionalism.

When you make it personal, you will lose every time.

This is a fact. I've heard too many stories of the indignant employee blowing his chances to get a raise, land a promotion or simply stay with the company. Remember what I said in Chapter 2: Your employer is a consumer looking for what he will get for his money. It's not about whether your boss likes you or finds you annoying. It is about proving your value to the company.

Here is the unfortunate tale of the maintenance manager plagued with the common symptoms of "management is against me" fever. This is another true story from a Fortune 500 food distribution and manufacturing company.

Kevin knew his plant like the back of his hand. He had been maintaining the plant for 25 years. He knew the history of the machines, and the technical support options for every area of the plant. When most people at the manufacturing plant had to spend hours troubleshooting how to fix equipment problems, Kevin had his own way of fixing things in a fraction of the time. Quietly, he would look at the equipment, list potential causes and conduct his own private troubleshooting sessions.

Kevin avoided training his subordinates at every opportunity. In his mind, management had been plotting to squeeze every bit of knowledge out of him, so they could replace him with a younger, cheaper worker. By keeping his knowledge to himself, Kevin believed he made himself more valuable to the company.

One day, Kevin politely asked his manager Eduardo for a raise. Eduardo reminded him that they had discussed the secrecy problems multiple times in the past. Time after time, Eduardo had stressed the importance of building up Kevin's team and sharing his knowledge to improve efficiency at the plant. He had also stressed that because of Kevin's strong technical skills, they wanted him to take on more responsibilities and climb up the ranks. But in order to do that, Kevin needed to delegate the lower level work to others.

As Eduardo explained management's position, Kevin tuned him out. He stopped listening, looked down at the floor and bit the inside of his cheeks as his resentment grew. Kevin walked out of the office feeling frustrated, powerless and even more convinced that management was plotting against him.

Did you see the huge discrepancy in how management interpreted Kevin's value and how Kevin saw his value? Management realized that Kevin possessed strong technical knowledge, but he wasn't adding much value to the company by keeping that knowledge to himself. On the other hand, Kevin thought he added value to the company by ensuring he was the only person who could do his job. He allowed his insecurities to distort his professionalism, which ended up threatening his job security rather than protecting it. If you were in Eduardo's position, how would you feel toward Kevin now?

Keep emotions out of it. Anything unrelated to your employer's priorities such as your personal reasons for wanting a raise or your feelings toward your boss or company have no role in this discussion. If you've become bitter or resentful about your current salary, do not display those emotions.

The "us versus them"—employees against management—mentality will always work against you. Recall the "employer as consumer" perspective held by the Fortune 500 HR manager in the introduction of this book. Your boss is searching for what the company—not you— can get out of the raise. There is no personal motive tied to that. You must provide your boss with a logical explanation of how the raise will benefit both you and the company. By doing that, you position yourself on the same side of the company.

If you're bitter and looking for a fight, how can you show your commitment to the company? It's simply not possible.

Prepare a meeting agenda or list of points.
At this point, you have an abundance of knowledge in your head. Now is the time to pick what information you will use and how you will use it. Each nugget of information supports your assertion that a raise will benefit both you and the company. Consider the information as supporting evidence of that point and prepare your notes accordingly.

Consider this a liquid draft throughout the preparation process. You will start with an outline and as you go through the tips in this chapter, you'll continually edit this agenda.

A written agenda helps in many ways:
- It allows you to present your arguments and supporting evidence in an organized fashion.
- It reminds you of points you might forget when facing your boss.
- It demonstrates your professionalism and respect for your boss's time.

Here is a very basic sample agenda:
I.   Personal assessment
     a. Your strong points, major accomplishments, your unique abilities
     b. Your weaknesses and how you plan to improve
II. Your local area salary findings
III. The company's growth in profit
IV. Next steps

This is only a sample agenda. You must tailor your agenda to your situation and present the strongest supporting evidence at the start of each point.

Tips on the Agenda Drafting Process

1) Keep your supporting information in perspective.
Don't get stuck on one fact or attach an emotion to that fact. If you do that, you risk losing focus. For example, let's say you discovered that your current salary was significantly below the salary of locals with similar positions. You feel as though you've been duped this whole time. You come into the meeting armed with this information, ready to tell the boss that it's unfair you've been getting paid so low. But you spend so much time discussing this point that you fail to mention some of your major accomplishments. The agenda will help you move on to your next points.

2) For each section of the agenda, make a note of your supporting evidence. List your strongest evidence first.

3) Prepare private notes for Plan B if your boss denies your request for a raise.

Remember this is a process rather than a single conversation with the boss. If your boss tells you that a raise is not possible now, you must be prepared to discuss what kind of plan you can formulate together that would benefit both you and the company.

Consider the following as you prepare your private notes:
- What additional responsibilities are you willing to take?
- What courses, books, seminars or conferences can you mention to the boss to enhance your skills or level of expertise?
- How long are you willing to work on these issues before getting the raise?

4) Practice, practice, practice. Role-play with a friend.

Speaking to the boss is altogether another skill. You need to practice saying the words out loud to another person. Listen to yourself. Ask your friend for a critique. Pick someone who will take this process seriously and not simply agree with whatever you say.

> At this point, you might become tempted to tell an office friend to help you with this. Who better to pretend to be the boss other than your office buddy who sees the boss every day, right? Wrong. Don't forget about the huge risks I mentioned in Chapter 4.

Brief your friend on your boss's personality. What points would your boss likely counter? What can you imagine him saying? Tell your friend as much as possible about your boss, so he or she can role-play effectively.

Try to anticipate every question, comment or counterpoint your boss will make. Ask your friend to say these aloud and address each one. You've already thought about this during your research in the previous chapter, but role-playing adds a higher level of preparation. It gives you the opportunity to hear potentially critical statements out loud and in turn, practice your professional responses out loud.

Encourage your role-playing partner to question and contradict every statement you make. This forces you to explain your points and edit out the points you cannot explain clearly. The more you practice, the more authority you will hold over that information and the more professional you will appear to the boss.

By the time you meet with the boss, you will easily keep your cool when he says, for example:

- You haven't proven yourself.
- The company cannot afford to give you a raise now.

- The person in your position never made that much. Why should you make more?
- What were you thinking?

5) Only bring the essentials.

The information you gathered in the previous steps will serve as your backup documentation. Feel free to bring neatly prepared notes, but do not bring so much paper to your meeting that it appears cumbersome.

Don't go over the top. Presenting too much information can be a big turnoff for the boss. Say, for example, that you discovered that your company has made steady profits by reading your company's annual report from the U.S. Securities and Exchange Commission website. Don't bring printed copies of each 50-page report for the last five years! If certain statistics from those reports are relevant to your discussion, write them down in your notes.

If you focus too much on presenting your backup documentation to the boss, you will lose your boss's attention. Know the information you are presenting. Don't rely solely on your notes. Keep your eye contact firm.

6) Prearrange the appointment.

This is not a suggestion or a "would-be-nice-if-you-did-this" tip. You must schedule the appointment ahead of time. Your boss will appreciate that you consider his time valuable. Don't expect to have your boss's undivided attention if you try to catch him in the hallway by saying, "Oh by the way, can we talk?" Even if you poke your head in the door and your boss says he is available, do not do take the impromptu meeting. A scheduled meeting is best.

Talk with the person who manages your boss's calendar and find out what is a good time of week and time of day. The more you know, the better. All managers have different internal clocks, so it's important that you know your boss's scheduling preferences (If you're familiar with his mood patterns, even better! You want him to be as agreeable as possible.) Some are early risers and prefer to meet with employees first thing in the morning when the office is quiet and less populated. Others prefer having one-on-one meetings toward the end of the day, when work is winding down and other meetings are over.

The meeting should be about 30 minutes and definitely no more than one hour. Your time and your boss's time are too valuable to let a meeting like this drag on longer than that.

If you approach the boss directly, be direct and simple, but don't explicitly mention you will ask for a raise. This is a perfectly respectable way to ask: Joe, I would like to meet when it's convenient for you to discuss my performance. What would be a good time for you in the next week or two?

If you ask in person, make sure no one else is around. Your boss will appreciate your professionalism in being discreet about this private matter.

Leave the ultimatums for the movies.

I admit it. When I was an employee, I sometimes fantasized about taking on a tough as nails persona with my boss. In the imagined scene, I would be standing at my boss's desk, looking him in the eye and saying with every ounce of bravado I could muster, "Give me a raise or I quit." He tries to read me, wondering whether or not to call my bluff. My penetrating glare tells him I'm dead serious. And then I say, "Go ahead . . . Make my day."

The boss suddenly realizes he can't let me walk out the door because if I did, the company would crumble. Later, I triumphantly describe the scene to my coworkers gathered around me, ending the story with, "And that's how I got my raise."

It's dramatic. It's forceful. But of course, that situation is mere fantasy. That's not how the real world works.

Ultimatums set you up for failure.

Once you threaten to quit, you better be prepared to face the consequences of losing that job. You've just put the dominos in motion in the worst way. There is no turning back from there. Your employer is more likely to accept your resignation because you've proven that your ego is more powerful than your common sense. You've also demonstrated your volatility. And no employer wants a loose cannon on the team.

Even if your ultimatum did succeed in forcing your boss to up your salary, your hostile approach will take its toll in the long run. That approach will ruin your relationship with the boss and may affect your chances for promotions in the future. When you obtain anything in life by threatening, the other side never has the same opinion of you again. You permanently taint your image in the other person's eyes.

Allow me to share a true story about a factory worker at a Fortune 500 food manufacturer and distributor. This story was relayed to me from a human resources manager at that company. Let's call the employee Roger, his supervisor Tom and the HR representative Tanya.

Overall, Roger was a hard worker. He came to work on time every day, finished his work and occasionally, he would surpass production goals. He took pride in his work. But Roger had a hot temper and any time something didn't go quite right, he would blow up at his coworkers. Those working alongside him grew weary of Roger's volatility and avoided communicating with him whenever possible.

His supervisor Tom was aware of this problem, but as an inexperienced manager, he had put off discussing it. He had hoped that by keeping his office door open at all times, all of his employees would feel comfortable talking with him about any problems in the factory.

One day, as Tom was scheduling shifts in his office, Roger walked in, noticeably ticked off. His nostrils flared and his eyes shot in different directions. He remained standing.

"I need a raise or I'm going to look somewhere else for a job," he said.

Tom instantly became concerned and proposed they both talk with the HR representative, Tanya. Tanya watched them standing outside her office window as she remained on a conference call. But as she sensed the tension, she excused herself from the call and let them in her office.

After Tom relayed the threat Roger had just made, Tanya reminded Roger of her previous discussion with him on his work performance and communication problems.

"What progress have you made on that?" she asked.

"I don't give a $#%! about that," Roger replied. "I do a better job than everyone else here." He explained that he had read in the newspaper the day before that the company had made record profits. According to Roger, the company was obligated to share those profits with its factory workers.

"We need to sit down and evaluate your performance at this point," Tanya replied.

But Roger wasn't having it. "I don't need to go through all this crap to get a stinkin' raise."

"Well then, Roger, I'm sorry that's the way you feel, but we're not giving you a raise."

"Fine, I quit."

And with that, Tanya accepted Roger's resignation, asked him for his keys and escorted him to his locker. Tom later told Tanya that he wasn't impressed with Roger's actions, but that he really needed Roger, since they were already short on that factory line.

But by then, it was too late. The resignation, Tanya explained, was non-negotiable. She also explained that Roger's attitude was beginning to influence other workers. Although Roger's skills would be missed, replacing Roger with someone possessing a better attitude needed to happen and would not be difficult.

I don't know Roger, but based on this story, he seemed to let his anger get the best of him. He may very well have been justified in asking for a raise. But his temper prevented him from having a productive conversation with his superiors. When Tanya probed, looking for the answer to "What is the company getting?" Roger failed to demonstrate his value. Any legitimate arguments he might have had were wiped out by his hostility and lack of preparation, presentation and professionalism.

CHAPTER 6
The Meeting

You're at the homestretch. Remember that the ultimate goal of this conversation is proving your worth to the company. As I mentioned in Chapter 2, your employer wants to know what she would get for her money. Show her that a raise would buy a bright, hardworking professional with even more to offer since your hire date or last raise.

At this point, you're coming into the conversation more prepared than most employees who ask for a raise. The previous chapters have given you a strong foundation that has hopefully boosted your confidence. Most importantly, the preparation has helped you know yourself better—and that will be the key to getting the most out of this meeting.

This chapter will guide you through the typical salary discussion and provide suggested lines for you in italics. This is not a script for you to memorize. I offer them to you to show that you have the power to steer this meeting into a positive and productive discussion, regardless of your employer's responses. The lines also convey the professional and relaxed tone behind the statements in an employee's voice.

I have also scattered several tips throughout this chapter. All of them apply for the entire meeting, but I have placed them in the segments I felt would be most helpful to you.

Before we get into the weighty tips that make you go "Hmmm," here are the quickies:

- Arrive five minutes early.
- Be flexible with scheduling the meeting.
- Annunciate.
- Look your boss in the eye.
- Sit up straight.

As you head into the meeting, here are the four "megatips" you must remember. I call them megatips because each one is multidimensional and goes a long way.

Tip #1: Think of the big picture.

This is one meeting out of many over the course of your entire career. You're meeting with one of the many bosses you will have in your life. The walls will not come crashing down if it doesn't go as well as you had hoped. The worst that will happen is you don't get a raise. And if that happens, you will use this meeting to guide you to getting a raise in the future.

Tip #2: Be yourself—your most professional self.

The first time I heard "be yourself," it was my first day of school and I was worried I wouldn't make any friends. When I allowed myself to just be me, I let my guard down and that vulnerability attracted friends. This age-old advice seems to help everything fall into place in many situations. When you're asking for a raise, being genuine benefits you in several ways:

- It relieves the tension on both sides of the conversation. On the other hand, if you put on a facade, your boss will detect it, which will make both of you uncomfortable and guarded.

• When you allow your boss to see you as a person beyond the employee, you make yourself vulnerable. That, in turn, allows your boss to do the same. When both sides have their guards down, they can communicate most effectively.

• Wherever the conversation goes, being yourself will keep you grounded.

Tip #3: Your boss is a normal person. Do not allow yourself to feel intimidated.

The relationship you have with your boss impacts your ability to be yourself. If you put your boss on a pedestal, do not know him well, or simply dislike him, you may find it difficult to follow Tip #2. So I offer an alternative tidbit to help you be yourself: Your boss is a normal person. Your boss puts his pants on one leg at a time just like everyone else. His role as your boss is merely his function in the company. Just like your boss, you have your own function in the company. No matter where you fit in the hierarchy, there should be a basic level of mutual respect.

Tip #4: Engage in the conversation.

In previous chapters, I emphasized the importance of preparation. Preparation will give you plenty of substantive insights to offer, whereas, lack of preparation will lead you to grasp at straws. But don't let that preparation prevent you from actively participating in the conversation. This is what I don't want to happen:

You've done your research, role-played, and drafted a killer agenda. As you enter your boss's office, you are making eye contact, but in your head, you're going over everything you practiced. As you sit down, you're clutching the agenda in your hands, trying to figure out how to cover every detail in 30 minutes. Your boss starts talking and you worry she will go off on a tangent when she discusses the future of the company, her vision for your future in the company, or anything slightly off topic.

Just relax! Listen. Stay in the moment. Keep an open mind. When you engage in the conversation and show your genuine concern for the company and your career, your boss will reciprocate. Your boss sees your function in the company from a larger perspective than you do. You might be pleasantly surprised at the insights she has into your abilities. Remember Kevin, the maintenance manager, in Chapter 5? His managers had discussed among themselves his potential to move up in the company. His managers had tried explaining that to him several times, but because Kevin was fearful his managers wanted to get rid of him, he never heard the message.

Consider this meeting a conversation with a reciprocal exchange. Glean every bit of wisdom, insights, and information you can get from the boss. Throughout your career, your listening and observational skills will move you forward, including in your quest for a raise.

Part I: Your Introduction

Thank you for taking the time to meet with me today. I know that your time is limited and valuable, so I brought an agenda.

I really enjoy working here and I appreciate the opportunity you've given me. I look forward to taking on new challenges with my position and I enjoy working with you.

> Showing your appreciation for the job sets a pleasant, cordial tone to the discussion. Make sure to include that at the opening of the conversation.

When I took this position, my intent was to grow in my role, contribute my skills to the team and make a difference. Over the last few weeks, I've spent a lot of time outside work analyzing my performance, looking at areas that need improvement and thinking about how I'd like to continue growing. I believe that I've done very well and exceeded the expectations of the job. With this in mind, I'm requesting an increase in my salary. What are your thoughts?

> **Tip #5: Open-ended questions are your friend. Use them throughout the discussion.**
> Open-ended questions spur more conversation, as they cannot be answered by a quick yes or no. Here's an example: A poor clothing salesman will ask the question, "Do you want to buy a suit today?" The shopper feels trapped because she can only respond with "yes" or "no." A good salesman will ask, "What type of suit are you interested in?" This question compels the other party to engage in further conversation.

After your introduction, open-ended questions such as "What are your thoughts?" or "What do you think?" put the ball back in the boss's court.

It gives your boss room to digest the information you just presented and respond on her terms. The question is so open, so unassuming, that it poses no threat. Your boss is then free to direct the conversation from here. For your boss, having that control is a good feeling.

Later in this chapter, we will address other areas of the meeting where open-ended questions can be effective.

Tip #6: In any negotiation, give wiggle room to the other side.
Let's say you took the opposite approach and asked very bluntly, "Can I have a raise?" or "Can you give me a raise?" or worse, "I think I deserve a raise. Don't you?" This is the equivalent of cornering a caged animal. (Yes, I know your boss is not an animal. He may have his dark moments when he loses his temper, but I promise he is not an animal.) By approaching this sensitive topic in an abrasive manner, you are exerting unnecessary force and the results will be highly unpredictable.

On the other hand, when you give wiggle room to the other side, there is very little chance the other side will respond with hostility.

Tip #7: Talk the talk: Use "we" and "us"
Language is an extremely powerful tool. If you use it effectively, it can break down barriers. You want to get

the message across that you and the boss are on the same side. For example, if you're proposing a plan to work toward a future raise, use the phrase, "Let's do this . . . " It projects the idea and reinforces your belief that both you and your boss are in this together.

In Chapter 5, I warned against having the "us against them" mentality. Show your boss that you consider yourself an extension of the company through your language. Demonstrate that you are invested in the company's success.

Tip #8: Silent pauses are okay.
I understand silence can feel awkward, especially in a discussion with your boss over salary. But remember this: You are asking for a raise because you've come to an informed conclusion that you deserve one. Be comfortable with that.

Just as you give room to the boss whenever you ask "What are your thoughts?" offer the same room to silent pauses. Let them happen. Your boss is most likely pondering your statements. Stay present in the moment. Don't let your mind wander or try to read into whether the silence is good or bad. Simply wait for your boss to make his next statement.

If you're inclined to fill in the silence by saying something, bite your tongue or count to ten slowly in your head. In a situation like that, you will most likely say something out of nervousness and that will not help you.

Part II: Your Assessment

Explain the personal assessment you completed in Chapter 3. Make sure to discuss both your strengths and weaknesses. By showing the boss that you are aware of your weaknesses, it shows your proactive approach to improving your performance. Your boss will appreciate that and you'll likely set yourself apart from 90% of the other employees that have requested salary increases.

> **Tip #9: Use your agenda for support.**
> Your printed list of points in hand will be your savior at several points in the conversation. Keep it close at all times during the meeting so you can continually refer back to it. However, do not follow the agenda so rigidly that you miss out on valuable exchanges with your boss. Don't forget Tip #4: Engage in conversation.
>
> •   If you get nervous and forget something you wanted to say, stick to the agenda.
>
> •   If you get frustrated that the conversation is not going the way you planned, stick to the agenda.
>
> •   If your boss goes off on a tangent that is not helpful to this conversation or your career development, interrupt politely and let him know that you value his time and would like to have enough time to address all the points in the agenda.

Part III: Dollar Figures

If your boss is open to granting your request for a salary increase, she will typically lead the conversation into dollar amounts. She'll ask your expectations for a raise. If you've followed the steps in the previous chapters, this will be easy to address. You've already prepared for this.

You answer that question with facts. Present your findings from your research on what others in your position typically earn. If applicable, talk about competency levels of others in similar positions and how you surpass those.

Then you put that information in your boss's lap like so:
I've found this company to be very fair in the past, so I'm confident that you'll propose a fair amount. What are your thoughts?

> **Reminder of Tip #5: Open-ended questions are your friend.**
> By presenting the market value information to the boss and then asking an open-ended question, you're continuing to cultivate a cordial environment. You've shared your research, but you are still not demanding a certain amount. The open-ended question hands over control to the employer much more effectively than if you were to say, "I want a 30% raise."

Part IV: Your Employer Responds

If she offers lower than you expected . . .

I'll be honest with you. I had hoped for more. Would you help me understand where I didn't hit the mark? It's not that I don't appreciate the offer. I really do. But based on my research, I was hoping for more. Where are some of the areas I need to improve? What can we do to get my salary closer to my expectations?

If she needs to confer with the higher-ups . . .

Sure, no problem. I certainly understand your position. When should I expect a response from you?

If she says no . . .

Remain calm. Remember, it all comes back to preparation, presentation and professionalism.

> **Tip #10: Offer a few suggestions on how you can increase your value in a specific timeframe.**
> You prepared for this in earlier chapters. Now is the time to offer them. Tell your boss the various options you have considered in order to make a salary increase a viable option:
>   • taking on more responsibilities
>
>   • attending a course, conference, seminar or special training
>
>   • completing a project

> • reaching a certain level of sales goals, production goals, customer service satisfaction goals
>
> By setting the specific time period, it helps both of you work toward a goal. You can schedule and prioritize the items on your list. Naming the plan gives it even more of a foundation. For example, if your time period is 90 days, call it the "90 day performance enhancement plan."

There are plenty of reasons your boss could reject your request for a salary bump. Here are some of the various explanations and how you can begin to respond to them:

1) "The company is going through financial difficulties."
Yes, I am aware of this. May I pose a suggestion? As I mentioned, my desire is to make a difference in this company. How would you feel about setting up an action plan together to help me improve and at some point, help me get a raise? Would it be possible for me to accept additional responsibilities in order to increase my pay? May I suggest we explore the possibility of raising my salary in smaller increments? How about we revisit this issue six months from now, when the company is hopefully doing better?

2) "Company policy only allow raises to be given once a year."
I thought that might be the situation. May I make a suggestion? As I mentioned, my desire is to make a difference in this company. How would you feel about setting up an action plan together to help me improve and at some point, help me get a raise? Would it be possible for me to accept additional responsibilities in order to increase my pay upon the year anniversary of my hire date?

3) "You don't deserve a raise."

I appreciate your time. Are there areas that you feel I could improve upon, so that when we revisit this topic, it can have a different outcome? How would you feel about setting up an action plan together to help me improve and at some point, help me get a raise? What areas do you see me excelling in?

At this juncture, stay positive no matter how difficult it may be. Even if your boss is bringing you down with negative feedback, avoid the tendency to become defensive, blame others, or whine about why you have trouble getting your work done. That reaction will only decrease your value in the eyes of your employer. A valuable employee is able to confront problems and take criticism.

If you're having a difficult time deciding what to say after your boss has given you negative feedback, you can say this: *Let me think about that and I'll get back to you.* This allows you to tuck it away for later and continue the meeting. Give yourself time to absorb that feedback.

> **Remember Tip #1: Think of the big picture.**
> If your boss is showing signs that he is not willing to compromise or work with you on a long-term plan to help you get a raise, you need to think privately about whether you want to continue working for this employer.
>
> I've known many people who get down on themselves and fall into a funk for several weeks after meeting with the boss. They lose concentration and their work performance noticeably plummets. In some cases, those people have gotten fired.

> Ask yourself: Do I want to stay at this company? What do I want out of this job? Is it helping or harming my career to stay here? Does the culture foster growth among the employees? If I stay at this company, should I try to transfer to another department? Is my boss keeping me from progressing?
>
> No matter what you decide to do, you must continue doing your best work until your last day. Don't burn your bridges.

Part V: Thank Your Employer

I appreciate everything you've said. Thank you for the feedback and taking the time to meet with me.

Part VI: Follow Up in Writing

Regardless of how your meeting goes, it's always best to follow up with a quick email or personal note thanking your boss again for meeting with you. Include what you agreed upon to avoid any confusion or misunderstanding in the future.

CHAPTER 7
Design a Plan

Okay, so your boss didn't immediately grant your request for a raise. That doesn't equate rejection, failure, or a waste of time. If he agreed to work with you on a plan to move you in the right direction, consider it a small victory. That means he listened to you and appreciated your professional approach to asking for a raise.

You might be frustrated, disappointed, or angry that you didn't get the raise right away. How are you going to handle it? By sulking? Fuming? Going home early? Bah! You're just fine because you already prepared for this in Chapter 5. Use your energy toward designing an effective plan to get that raise.

Call it a "performance enhancement plan," a "professional development plan," a "salary boost plan," or simply "the plan." Call it whatever excites you. (In front of your boss, call it whatever he wants to call it.)

"Even a 1,000 mile journey starts with a single step." —Lao Tzu

This plan will outline the steps toward your goal. Consider your timeframes for each step and decide whether it's appropriate to ask for small, incremental raises throughout the plan or one raise at the end of the plan. Throughout the plan drafting process, consider how you and your boss or a manager will hold you accountable.

Below are more questions to help you get started. You will have to tailor your plan to your position, company, boss and most importantly, your own career goals. There is no rule that you must create an intricate plan or a simple plan spanning a certain period of time. You determine what works best for you. Oftentimes, the simpler, the better.

> **Undersell. Over deliver.**
> Salespeople have most likely heard this golden piece of advice. In my decades-long career, this one tip has helped me tremendously, and I can't think of a better time to share it with you. When money is on the line and you're thinking of how to increase your value, it's natural to think big. You want that extra money and you want to make an offer your boss can't refuse. I encourage you to be optimistic and ambitious, but remember to be realistic. Your plan is only as good as your ability to follow through. Empty promises to your boss will only decrease your value. Remember, it is better to deliver above expectations rather than disappoint with underachievement.

Training
- What do you want to learn?
- Are there specific books or other reference materials you must read and study?
- In your line of work, what certifications or licensing must you obtain? What tests must you take to move up to higher paying positions or make you more competitive in your industry?
- Are there seminars, courses or conferences you should attend?
- Clarify with your employer whether this training must be done during work hours or personal time.

- Clarify with your employer if the company will pay for these training activities partially or in full.
- Don't expect your employer to have all the answers. Do your own research. In the Internet age, you have limitless sources of information and technology that allows you to learn from your computer.
- Search for training opportunities like conference calls, webinars, or workshops you can easily fit in your work schedule. Somewhere in the world, there is a free event being conducted by a successful leader in your industry.
- Troll for industry insider blogs and get on the mailing lists for newsletters, white papers and anything else that will keep you informed about your industry, trade, or profession.

Networking is a great way to find training opportunities.

Having a community or network of people who share an interest in your line of work is priceless. Use social networking sites like <u>Meetup</u> or <u>LinkedIn</u> to find the groups that can help you. You'll be surprised at the wealth of supportive, online communities and the valuable exchange of information, including training. Join trade associations or just get on their mailing lists to receive notices of training events.

Mentoring

Does a mentor arrangement fit with your workplace culture? Is your boss open to facilitating this type of relationship with you and a manager? Pairing up with a mentor—especially another staffer with more experience and knows your position particularly well—can be a meaningful experience. This person can coach you, check in with you and hold you accountable to keep you on track with your plan. This mentor might have been in your position in the past or witnessed the company's ups and downs in the last decade. Even shadowing your mentor on a few occasions may benefit you. Because this person is not your direct supervisor, there is less pressure to impress and more room to be yourself. Most importantly, your mentor has the advantage of understanding the politics of your workplace and can become your strongest ally and cheerleader within your company.

You might also consider hiring a personal career coach. Many employees, as well successful executives, have hired personal coaches to help them raise their performance levels and reach career objectives.

Volunteering

If you're hungry for experience in a certain area but your company doesn't allow newbies to dabble in it, look for a nonprofit or any other organization that needs volunteers doing that type of work. Inform your boss and see if you can incorporate volunteer work in your plan.

Teamwork

Will joining a team at your workplace enrich your experience or sharpen your skills at the company?

New Responsibilities

Are you open to supervising or mentoring a junior coworker? Will that make life easier for your boss?
What new responsibilities can you take over?
What specific tasks can you add to your routine?

Setting Goals

S.M.A.R.T. is a well-known mnemonic used to set goals. Hundreds of websites reference this mnemonic, which first appeared in a 1981 issue of Management Review by George T. Doran.

- Specific
- Measurable
- Attainable

- Relevant
- Time-bound

Every goal you set should pass the S.M.A.R.T. test before you present it to the boss. Here are some examples of underdeveloped goals from various industries that I have reformulated.

Original Goal	S.M.A.R.T. Goal
In no time, my sales figures will be among the top in the region.	Within two months, I'll increase my sales by 25%.
Within five months, I'll land some elite accounts.	Within five months, I'll land four more accounts with Fortune 500 companies.
Within a few months, I'll be entering data faster than ever!	Within three months, I'll raise my typing speed to 80 words per minute.
Within six months, I'll have conducted enough experiments to find the missing link.	Within six months, I'll have conducted the three experiments using the high-grade epoxy.
Within 30 days, our brand will go viral!	Within two weeks, I'll have established an online presence for the company through new accounts in multiple forms of social media. Within three months, I'll have attracted 50,000 Twitter followers to the company's account.

I'll see to it that you don't hear any more complaints about the accounting department.	Within two months, my accounting team will be processing checks within two weeks of receiving the invoice.
As soon as I get through this audit, I'll have a better handle on marketing.	Within four months, my two top priority marketing projects will be ready for your review.

Allow yourself to write down all the possibilities. Be creative. Imagine yourself in new roles. Don't edit yourself until later. Even if a potential new task sounds unappealing, write it down. You may later think of a way to benefit from that added task or responsibility.

Take a lesson from football. Build a safety valve into your plan.

Even the most well-designed football plays crafted by the top coaches need a backup plan. When the quarterback looks for his intended receiver and discovers the defense has him covered, the quarterback has to throw the ball to his Plan B, the secondary receiver. Notice that the quarterback doesn't frantically search for just anyone. The secondary receiver is always built into the plan.

Do the same for your plan. When you talk with the boss about implementing the plan, be sure to include something like this: *If I get the feeling I'm in over my head, would it be okay if we talked about this again?* This painless, unassuming statement can be your cushion later if you feel the need to scale back your added responsibilities.

Reality check

Once you've written down all the possibilities, do a reality check with the following questions covering logistics:

- Can this plan work given the company culture, the industry, your boss's work style?
- If you follow this plan, how much extra time each week will it take? Are you committed to putting in the additional hours?
- Is it necessary to build flexibility into this plan? If yes, talk with your boss about how to do that.
- Will delegating some of your duties to another colleague free up your time to follow through on this plan? Will your boss allow you to do that? Will your boss assign you someone to delegate to? Is now a good time of the year to start this plan or should you wait until the busy season ends? One way to determine that is to write out all of your priorities for each month. Be intimately familiar with the busy and slow seasons.

> **Get it in writing.**
> When you meet with your boss to discuss the design and implementation of the plan, request a written statement showing the expectation of the anticipated promotion or salary. If your company's legal department does not allow this, make a point to your boss that you will follow through on the plan based on good faith. Also request that human resources keep the plan in your personnel file for future reference.

CHAPTER 8
Ready, Set, Go

What are you doing now? Are you staring at this plan feeling woozy, wondering what the heck you've gotten yourself into? This is not the time to doubt yourself. Keep the momentum going and, like Nike says, "Just do it."

When you designed the plan in the last chapter, you were thoughtful, creative, introspective. This step is where the rubber meets the road, where you sink or swim, where you show what you're made of. Your boss has heard you and given you the chance to add more value to the company. She has entrusted you with heavier responsibilities and the company overall now has a stake in your success.

This plan started with your goal to increase your salary, but by now, I'm sure you know it's about much more than a paycheck. It's about you. Prove it to yourself that you can do this. Yes, you may be motivated because of your commitment to your boss, your coworkers and your company, but ultimately, you'll stay motivated if you realize that you are doing this to improve yourself.

The Proactive Professional Always Wins

Unfortunately, the word "proactive" is a buzz word in career development circles, similar to "a gamer" or "outside-the-box thinker." From my experience getting to know hundreds of job seekers, I know these buzz words can actually be a turn-off. They're difficult to place in context in relation to your day-to-day life. But allow me to explain "proactive" simply, as Merriam-Webster Dictionary defines it: acting in anticipation of future problems, needs or changes.

You will have to be proactive in order to succeed in this next phase.

But Russ, that's just not me! I don't have a proactive bone in my body.

If you've followed the steps in this book so far, whether you realize it or not, you've been proactive this whole time! You assessed yourself before your boss mandated a companywide performance evaluation; you put together supporting backup before asking for a raise; you even prepared a strategy to respond to potential resistance from your boss before the meeting.

The proactive steps you have taken so far set this plan in motion. On the other hand, the reactive person—the opposite of the proactive person— would have sat back and waited for something to happen.

Humor me for a moment as I demonstrate the difference between the proactive person and the reactive person.

Mildred, The Reactive Employee	Miranda, The Proactive Professional
Is five minutes late to many meetings because she often books herself in back-to-back meetings	Is rarely late to meetings. She allows herself 15 minutes in between meetings in case one meeting goes long.

Runs to the office supply store when she discovers toner is out. Her coworkers wait anxiously to print.	Buys toner regularly and always has extra toner cartridges stocked in the cabinet near the printers. Has informed her coworkers where to find them, so they can refill toner when she is unavailable.
Has loads of work waiting for her when she returns from vacation. During one recent vacation, her email inbox filled up so quickly, the server rejected the last 20 emails.	Worked an extra seven hours a week for two weeks before her planned vacation. She notified all of her contacts she would be out of the office, so nobody emailed her while she was out.
Chases down her coworkers for their lunch orders a few minutes before they walk into the weekly lunch meeting.	Emails her coworkers with the menu the night before the weekly meeting and gives them a deadline to respond via email.

Both Mildred and Miranda have a lot of work. But who do you think is more stressed out? Mildred lets the job run her. Miranda runs her job. I'm sure it took Miranda a while to master her work habits. She must have gone through some trial and error before developing her methods. Without a doubt, Miranda learned that being proactive made her more effective. She also learned that after she formed certain habits, being proactive became second nature to her.

Now let's look at an example of higher level executives that either react or are proactive.

Ken, The Reactive Exec	Rob, The Proactive Exec
Advises subordinates of the need to meet to discuss upcoming changes, then advises that he is too busy to have the meeting. He says things will have to remain the same until he can find time to think about possible solutions.	Advises subordinates of the need to meet to discuss upcoming changes. Solicits coworkers for possible solutions. Emails agenda to participants two days prior to the meeting, and asks attendees to consider recommendations to bring to the meeting.
Believes that no one can do the job better than he. He tries to handle all his travel arrangements, fields every customer call, makes each customer delivery, but complains to his boss that there is no time in the day for more business development. His sales remain stagnant.	Builds teams of trusted subordinates by assigning them responsibility to engage with current customers and answer their questions and make his travel arrangements. He rotates his staff weekly to make deliveries, so customers always see a familiar face. He spends better than half of his day on new business development. Sales continue to grow.

Are you reactive or proactive? Actions are driven by the habits we form.

Did you know 21 days is all you need?

It takes the average person 21 days to change old habits and form new ones. You must actively work on making new activities part of your routine for 21 consecutive days before it becomes as regular as brushing your teeth or taking a shower. After the twenty-first day, not only will the new habit become natural, you will feel like something is not right when you skip it.

Let me tell you about a story my friend Phil told me about forming a new habit.

Eight years ago, Phil's doctor gave him a stern warning that if he didn't start exercising, his heart health would quickly deteriorate. In the past, he had gone through spurts of regular exercise that would typically last a couple of weeks, but he was never able to stay consistent. The doctor's warning and an upcoming high school reunion motivated Phil to start jogging every day for 45 minutes.

He told me that waking up an extra hour early was extremely difficult in the beginning. He would set his alarm, press snooze a couple of times, and then discover it was too late to go. Then he set the alarm an hour and a half earlier, pressed snooze a couple of times, and woke up with enough time to jog. In the winter months, getting up before the sun came up and leaving his warm, cozy bed was torture. He wanted so badly to crawl back in bed and sleep as long as he could.

After the third week, his body became acclimated to the early alarm settings. He no longer needed to press the snooze button. His mind was more awake. Eventually, he stopped stumbling over his slippers in the morning. He had trained his body to wake up earlier. Interestingly, he says that on days he skips jogging, his legs cramp up.

Phil says he feels great and has a renewed vigor for life he never had before. It wasn't easy. But if you know that the light at the end of the tunnel is only 21 days away, I promise it will get easier. New habits can be a reality, but it starts with your desire.

Organizational skills will help you stay productive. Here are some tips that have worked for me:

1) Keep a pen and notebook with you at all times. Write down any good ideas that come to you, reminders, meetings to add to your calendar, things to tell your boss. Write down everything you might forget. If you prefer recording notes on a smartphone or other device, use whatever works best. From my experience, good old-fashioned pen and paper work better for me because the content is more visible. Writing memos to myself using apps on my smartphone makes it easy to ignore because once you close the app, the content is easily out of sight.

2) However, I do not discount the value of apps and I still encourage you to experiment with reminder/organizational apps and find which one helps you get organized. There are dozens of apps that come highly recommended by tech websites and consumer experts. I'm not listing any for three reasons: (1) I personally cannot vouch for one that I swear by; (2) there are too many

highly recommended apps for various devices; and (3) new apps come out every day. I would hate to list my top ten picks and have an even better app get released before you read this.

You can easily find the recommended apps by doing a search online for "best apps for organization." I encourage you to try different apps before sticking with one. Various methods work for different people, so it's definitely worth your while. Just don't get caught up trying them out that you never end up developing a system.

3) Use your online calendar. I use the Microsoft Outlook program, which allows me to set up automatic email reminders of upcoming events.

4) Keep a tickler file. I learned about this through a book by David Allen called *Getting Things Done*, but later learned the concept has been around much longer. In *Getting Things Done*, the tickler file is labeled by days. So for example, let's say the current month is March. You have one folder labeled 1, another labeled 2, and so on all the way to 31. File whatever paperwork you need to handle on each day appropriately. You also have a folder for each month. If something comes up that you need to remember in July, stick it in the July folder. On July 1, organize those papers by day in the numbered folders.

5) Always follow up with anybody you are requesting information from or working with. Don't rely solely on others to finish your project.

6) Be a stickler for details. Be punctual and keep your appointments. Your coworkers and clients will not want to work with you if

you're consistently late or forgetting meetings, deadlines or any other logistical details.

7) Every morning, before you leave home for the office, mentally check in with yourself. Are you embracing the day ahead or dreading it? Are you ready for the new challenges? Do you feel confident you can handle unexpected problems or issues that arise?

8) Every night, before you go to bed, ask yourself if you accomplished what you set out to do. If you didn't, don't beat yourself up. Simply put it on your list of priorities for the next day.

Ask yourself the deeper questions at least once a week and keep writing them down.

It is important to regularly check in with yourself by reviewing the questions in Chapter 3. In addition to those questions, ask yourself the following:

- How is the plan going so far?
- Am I able to cope with the additional time it takes to accomplish these goals?
- Are these goals realistic now that I'm working toward them?
- What am I learning from working toward these new goals?
- How can I apply the educational elements (workshops, classes, books) to my everyday life or to my future career goals?
- How have I changed since my first personal assessment before I asked for the raise?

Don't be afraid to ask yourself, "Do I really want this?"

You're pushing yourself and you deserve to be commended. You saw an area of your life that needed change (*i.e.* your paycheck) and you went out and tried to change it. But now that you're knee deep in the process, you have a more informed perspective. Ask yourself, "Am I enjoying this? Would I rather stay at my current rate of pay? Does this new job really fit me?"

Here's a story that illustrates my point.

Sammie was a stellar salesman for a specialty electronics distributor. He was bright, funny, warm, genuine and trustworthy. People liked him and gravitated to him. He could probably sell a typewriter to a web designer, a Jacuzzi to apartment dwellers, a heater in a tropical island. I'm not saying he was the slimy type who took advantage of people—he simply had an uncanny ability to talk to people and within five minutes, garner their attention, trust and curiosity. His customers loved him and continued coming back to him.

Sammie was ranked the top seller in his district for four years. So after a while, he felt the itch for a raise and promotion to regional manager.

When he reached that goal, Sammie got his promotion. Now his days were spent managing a team of six salespeople but not making a single sale himself. He got no satisfaction from being in the higher position. It felt more like babysitting and pushing paper to him. He missed the thrill of courting new customers, talking to new faces, and closing deals. Six months after the promotion, Sammie decided the regional manager position wasn't for him and asked to be demoted back to his original position and salary.

Some might question Sammie's decision since he left management to go back to the rank and file. However, Sammie's old customers were thrilled to have him back and recommended him to others. He had his old zest back. His sales increased. And his job satisfaction and income shot through the roof.

It happens in every industry: staff writers become editors, teachers become principals, lawyers become judges. You have a vision of what climbing up the ladder will be, but once you move up, you realize that you were happier in your previous position, where all the action was happening.

It is perfectly okay to come to this realization. In fact, it's great that you're realizing this now rather than later. You may worry what others will think of you. Sammie pondered the same question, but chose to be happy and fulfilled, rather than letting fear or pride stand in his way. As soon as you come to this conclusion, you must tell your superior right away. There is no use in dragging it out. The longer you wait, the more you risk doing poorly in your new position.

Check In Regularly With Your Boss

Schedule short regular meetings with your boss at least once a month. This gives you the opportunity to update your boss on your progress, concerns you have and any problems you might be experiencing. It also gives your boss the chance to give you feedback during the process rather than waiting for the very end of the period. I recommend monthly meetings because it gives you enough time to figure things out on your own and does not intrude on your boss's busy schedule.

These should be short touch-and-go meetings but are very important. With this feedback, you and your boss will be able to discern if you are on target and make adjustments to ensure that you meet the expectations established.

Be Honest If You're Struggling

In the previous chapter, I highlighted the importance of adding a "safety valve" to the discussion. If you're having a difficult time meeting the demands of your new responsibilities and are thinking about scaling back your plan, you must communicate that as soon as possible to your boss. Do not let this drag on! If you have overcommitted, be honest and address it . . . now!

Internalizing problems leads to procrastination, which leads to poor performance. Don't let your performance go sour. Talk to your boss. So maybe you discovered you weren't as strong in one area as you thought. Big deal. You would not have discovered that unless you did it. So now you know. Tell your boss. By now, you hopefully have a better relationship with your boss.

Think back to the safety valve and remember the tips from Chapter 6 on meeting with the boss. Schedule a meeting with the boss and simply tell him you'd like to talk about some problems you're having keeping up with the plan. Before meeting with him, think of some solutions you can present to help reduce your problem. Don't come crying to the boss without a proposed solution. Perhaps you need to delegate more duties. Perhaps you need to put off one project for another two months. Consider possible solutions and be open to hearing your boss's solutions.

You could say this: *My whole approach has not changed. I'm still motivated, but I feel like I'm really struggling in one area, and I need your input.*

Be prepared for the boss to mention the salary increase. He may change the amount of your potential raise originally agreed upon at the first meeting. Or he may tell you that you may not get the raise at all. Remember not to take it personally. Whatever figure you both discussed previously was predicated on the assumption that you would follow through with the plan. Now that you cannot follow through, you must face the reality that it may affect your potential salary increase. If it doesn't, then all the better for you.

CHAPTER 9
The Final Meeting

Preparing for the final meeting with your boss will be similar to the kind of preparation you have already done before, except with less research. Go through the same questions in the personal assessment in Chapter 3. With each of these also ask yourself, how have I changed since I first asked myself these questions? Recap what you have accomplished and what you have struggled with. Think very deeply about the transformation you went through during this period.

Review your notes from your more personal assessments and any notes you might have taken from your check-in meetings with your boss. Do these notes tell a story? Write a statement of how you have grown, improved or learned from this experience. Regardless of what you've accomplished, you have improved your overall understanding of the business, your skills and the skills that you'll need in the future.

Now review chapter 5 and 6 to help you get into the proper mindset for the final meeting. However, this final meeting is very different from the first meeting you had. There is no research you need to do aside from your own self-assessment. If you've followed through on the plan, then it's very likely you'll get the raise.

Be ready for good news. Be ready for bad news.

If you get the raise, congratulations! It's what you set out to do and you succeeded. Be thankful and express your heartfelt appreciation to your employer. Make it clear that you're excited to contribute to the team and continue growing with the company.

You can always go through the same process of asking for a raise in the future. Whether you're an hourly employee, a mid-level manager or a top-level executive, the process in this book is the most professional and effective method in asking for a salary increase.

If the boss offers you a raise lower than you expected—or worse, none at all—stay calm. Put a smile on your face, hold your head up high and tell your boss that you appreciate his consideration. You may tell your boss that although you do not totally understand his position, you accept his decision. Let him know that you intend to continue growing in your position and would like to be considered for a raise in the future. Thank him for his time and for working with you on the plan.

But Russ, how can you expect me to stay calm? I've just spent the last six months working my tail off! I've followed every step in this book. I woke up at the crack of dawn most mornings just to read books, blogs, trade publications, and reference materials. I missed out on movie nights and dinner dates to work late and put out fires at the office. I even missed a concert! And I picked up a bad coffee habit just to get me through the

day. Now I know what they mean by "blood, sweat and tears." I gave it my all—and I got nothin.'

Ok, so you probably feel like you got punched in the stomach. Naturally, getting your request turned down after all your hard work will seem unfair, disappointing, and leave you feeling somewhat hopeless. But just because you didn't get the raise, does that really mean you "got nothin?" Of course not! Go somewhere private. Now, name five new skills you picked up. Name three successful projects you executed. Name five new co-workers who have greater respect for you. Name 10 specific tasks you can do better, faster and with more authority.

Get the idea? You've gained more than you know. Going through the process in this book provided you with a tremendously valuable experience. Admit it. You are better off having gone through the process.

If you don't believe me, update your resume. Go ahead, add your new skills, responsibilities and areas of expertise on your resume. Do you have a professional website? Add everything to your site as well. You've just increased your competitive edge ten-fold.

Also, have you considered the impression you've left on your coworkers and other managers? These people may be valuable members of your professional network in the future. They may be future clients, employers or coworkers at a different company. Remember Tip #1 from Chapter 6: Think of the big picture. This is one job out of many you will have in your career.

You came into this process knowing that ultimately, your employer would have the final say on whether or not you got that raise. Part of being your most professional self is being able to take criticism and learning from it.

Whether you get the raise or not, resist all temptation to tell a coworker.

I warned you in Chapter 4 against confiding in an officemate, and I warn you again. At this point, you're either feeling ecstatic or down in the dumps. Either way, you'll feel a sudden urge to share your story. Don't do it!

Allow me to illustrate using Randy and Ronald, employees at a top insurance company, working in the same building.

Randy met with his boss on a late Friday afternoon. He was almost sure the time slot meant his boss would deliver some bad news. To his surprise, his boss told him he was getting a raise. *Yippee!!* Randy's shoulders went limp, as if the news had literally lifted a weight off of them. He walked out of the boss's office with a big silly grin.

"What's with you?" his cubicle neighbor Lily asked. Lily, amused and curious, had never seen Randy this happy. His smile was infectious and she found herself smiling as she asked him.

"I got a raise!" Randy blurted out. Just as the four words left his mouth, he saw the smile on Lily's face drop. For a few short seconds, she seemed stunned.

"Congratulations," she said, trying hard to concentrate. Lily made a concerted effort to be gracious and smile again. Of course, even a forced smile was difficult to pull off when she was thinking, *Good for you! I've been asking for a raise for four months now and I haven't had your luck. I guess it always pays to be chummy with the boss. No wonder you've been Mr. Helpful recently! You were only looking out for No. 1.*

Not surprisingly, Lily lost respect for Randy and her resentment against him grew. She complained to her friend and coworker Tina, another disgruntled employee who had long felt that she was underpaid. By the end of the week, Randy's six-person department knew about his raise and they all resented him for earning more money than they did.

Six floors down in the same building, Ronald had just left a meeting with his boss in another department. He could feel his heart pounding and the temples surrounding his forehead throbbing. His boss had just informed him he would not get the raise he had requested. Ronald wanted to go back to his cubicle, pack up and never come back. But he knew he couldn't quit. He needed this job to support his two kids. I've given 10 years to this miserable company and this is the thanks I get, he thought.

Ronald walked slowly to his desk in a daze. He felt defeated. There was no hurry to do anything for the rest of the day.

"Hey Ronnie, what's wrong?" his buddy Jim asked as he stopped him in the hallway.

"Just met with Smith. He wouldn't give me a raise."

"Aw, sorry, man." Jim had been with the company for five months and still learning the ropes. Technically,

Ronnie was one of Jim's supervisors.

They talked for a while in Ronnie's office with the door closed. For 30 minutes, Ronnie recounted every project, every success, and every sacrifice he ever made for the company. He told Jim how desperately he wanted to leave the company and how much he despised Smith, his supervisor. He told Jim every rumor he had heard about Smith's shady dealings.

After the first 10 minutes of Ronnie's rants, Jim began to feel uncomfortable. He hated gossip and questioned the legitimacy of the rumors. Jim waited for Ronnie to pause to make his exit. "It's getting late, Ronnie. I have to go. Tough break though."

A few weeks after that conversation, Ronnie assigned Jim a new project that would require them to work closely together under tight deadlines. Jim was hesitant. He knew Ronnie hated the company and was in a new mode of doing the least amount of work possible. He'll probably dump all the work on me and be a total flake, Jim thought.

Without Ronnie knowing, Jim purposefully took on another project from a different manager to block his schedule. Then, he politely declined Ronnie's assignment.

If you did not get the raise after having gone through the process laid out in this book, you need to consider whether or not this employer is the right fit for you.

Decision time: Should I stay or should I go?

This is a big decision. Remember back in Chapter 5 when I told you to leave emotions out of it? Now is another prime time to remember that. You must not let the volatile part of you dictate whether you stay or go. Deal with facts; do not let your anger, frustration, depression rule you. If you let your emotions rule, you'll most likely regret it.

A surefire way to make a rational, informed decision incorporates the Ben Franklin decision-making process. (This form is available on directionalmotivation.com.) I often use this method when I'm working with job seekers unsure of whether or not to pull the plug on their current jobs. Here is how it works. On a single piece of paper make two columns. Title the left column, "Reasons to stay" and the right column "Reasons to leave." Under each heading list the reasons for each, then compare them. Do not judge yourself for thinking one way or another. Do not let pride rear its ugly head as you draft these lists. Only you know what is best. Be completely honest with yourself.

Here's another exercise: If you had another job offer right now and it paid the same salary and was located the same distance from your home as your current job, what would you do?

Regardless of what you decide, remember that you have much more to offer than you did at the beginning of this process. If you decide to stay, you've most likely gained the respect of your coworkers and managers and are a stronger candidate for a promotion. Also, you'll be able to revisit the topic again. If you decide to leave, you can use your new skills to start fresh with a new employer.

CONCLUSION

If you went through the process outlined in this book, I commend you. You worked hard and took a no-nonsense, methodical approach to getting a raise. You were challenged to stay positive, patient, persistent and professional. Instead of letting frustration get the best of you, you worked on developing the best of you.

One of my objectives in this book was to show you the raise process from the employer's perspective. By understanding the concept that your employer is a consumer, you opened yourself up to a new perspective that allowed you to succeed. I hope that the workplace examples and probing questions throughout this book enabled you to develop the proper mindset going into the raise process. I also trust that this book has transformed your perspective, your value, and your future income potential.

Income is such a central part of life yet many people have a difficult time understanding how to take control of it. Many times throughout this book, I have stated and reinforced the idea that you have the power to create your value. This is true when you ask for a raise, aim for a promotion, interview for a new job, start a relationship, start a business, join a club and more.

I hope that this book has helped you with more than adding money to your bank account. My intention is to empower, challenge and excite you. If there is one overarching bit of wisdom you take away from this book, I hope it is this:

The little steps you take today will determine your future success.

The Directional Motivation series offers more resources to help you with your career and professional goals. Visit www.directionalmotivation. com to see our directory of products and services. Stay tuned for upcoming books, blogs, teleseminars, webinars, coaching programs, and other great content to help you get to the top of your game.

My desire for you is your continued success! You may have suggestions for additional topics that you would like me to address. Feel free to contact me at russ@directionalmotivation.com. I would love to hear from you.

The Directional Motivation series is continually adding new material to its library. But sometimes, the struggling employee needs more than just reading material. Hiring a career coach can be extremely beneficial to give you one-on-one attention, hold you accountable for your goals, and mentor you from outside your company. I provide career coaching services and offer a free 30-minute consultation over the phone. Please email me at russ@directionalmotivation.com for more information on my coaching services.

Of course, my only aim is to help you, not advertise my services. If you decide to shop around for a career coach, here are the key characteristics to look for in a coach:
- industry experience
- accessibility
- references
- compatible personalities
- reasonable cost

Most importantly, your career coach should aspire to help you reach your goals rather than his or her own.

A Final Thought

Always think in terms of the "Big Picture." Yes, I've said this multiple times throughout the book, but its importance here warrants repetition. Today's circumstances are only temporary. Take whatever workplace struggles you have experienced and use them to benefit you. Use that learned wisdom to manage your career. When you succeed in approaching your boss for a raise or tackling difficult workplace situations, you build character, business savvy, and most importantly, your own personal value.

Congratulations on your success.
I wish you even more success in the future.
—Russ Hovendick

"The little steps you take today will determine your future success."

RESOURCE GUIDE

Introduction
www.directionalmotivation.com

Chapter 4
www.salary.com
www.payscale.com
www.bls.gov/ooh/
www.bloomberg.com
www.google.com/finance
finance.yahoo.com
http://www.sec.gov/edgar/searchedgar/companysearch.html
http://www.sec.gov/investor/pubs_subject.shtml#fstatements

Chapter 7
www.meetup.com
www.linkedin.com

Chapter 8
Allen, David. *Getting Things Done: The Art of Stress-Free Productivity.* New York: Penguin Books, 2001.

ABOUT THE AUTHOR

Russ Hovendick is a national award winning executive recruiter. For 20 years, he has motivated hundreds of people through his multiple roles as recruiter, career coach, business owner, and volunteer chaplain/counselor within the Jail and Prison System of South Dakota. He heads *Client Staffing Solutions, Inc.,* an executive recruiting agency, and recently founded the *Directional Motivation Group*, which offers career development books, training, coaching services, and resources.